First Steps out of Anxiety

Why this book?

- Do you, or does a loved one, suffer from anxiety?

Do you find that

- you worry constantly, feel restless, or have trouble concentrating?
- you are irritable and on edge?

Anxiety is a very common problem, but despite its prevalence many people don't understand it. Most importantly, they don't understand that it *can* be managed – anxiety doesn't have to rule your life.

This book explains:

- what anxiety is and how it works;
- what provokes it and what makes it worse;
- what you can do to control it;
- how to overcome it when it does happen.

Although no one's life can ever be completely anxiety-free, you can control how much power anxiety has – taking steps towards a happier, healthier you.

This book is dedicated to the people who have been brave enough to challenge and overcome their anxiety – and who have given me the privilege of sharing that journey with them. I hope your bravery inspires others as much as it has inspired me.

First Steps out of Anxiety

Dr Kate Middleton

LION

A Lion Book
an imprint of
Lion Hudson plc
Wilkinson House, Jordan Hill Road,
Oxford OX2 8DR, England
www.lionhudson.com
ISBN 978 0 7459 5519 3

Distributed by:
UK: Marston Book Services, PO Box 269,
Abingdon, Oxon, OX14 4YN
USA: Trafalgar Square Publishing, 814
N. Franklin Street, Chicago, IL 60610
USA Christian Market: Kregel Publications,
PO Box 2607, Grand Rapids, MI 49501
First edition 2010
10 9 8 7 6 5 4 3 2 1 0

Acknowledgments
p. 84: Extract from *Harry Potter and the
Prisoner of Azkaban* – Copyright ©
J. K. Rowling 1999.

A catalogue record for this book is available
from the British Library
Typeset in 10.5/14 ITC Stone Serif
Printed and bound in Malta

Contents

Introduction

Anxiety is everywhere. If you think about the emotions you experience, anxiety is probably one of those you experience most often. Anxiety exists across all cultures and all age groups. It is one of the first emotions seen in small babies, and it is present in all kinds of other animals. Unfortunately, anxiety is also one of the most problematic emotions. It is one of the most unpleasant to experience and often the one that makes us feel the most out of control.

Did you know?

- Clinically, anxiety is related to more different mental health conditions than any other emotion.
- Anxiety can become a long-term, chronic problem and can restrict people's lives and lead to other issues as people try to find ways to cope with the unpleasant symptoms they are feeling.
- Anxiety doesn't just affect the way you feel emotionally – it has physical consequences too,

with an array of health problems caused, worsened by, or linked to anxiety.

- Anxiety is a growing problem – one study in 2009 found that more than a third of people reported feeling more anxious than they used to.

As you are reading this book, you probably know all too well how quickly anxiety can become your enemy – and how it can grow and start to take over your life. Once you are in the grip of anxiety, it can feel merciless and impossible to escape. But it *is* possible to overcome your anxiety and get back in control.

The truth is that no one can ever be totally anxiety-*free* – anxiety has too crucial a role in controlling and influencing your behaviour, and without it you would be in danger, unable to respond quickly enough to risks or blundering into situations without seeing them coming. But you can greatly reduce the amount of anxiety you have to deal with, and become better at coping when those nervous moments do kick in. This book is all about helping you to understand your anxiety better and stopping it from taking over your life – how to take those first steps and win back some ground from anxiety!

Remember, like all emotional conditions, anxiety can be a serious problem. This book will walk you through the first steps in tackling anxiety, but if your anxiety levels are very high, or if your anxiety is making you think or act in ways that worry you or those around

you, you may find that you need more support. Make sure you also talk things over with your doctor. Most of all, though, don't despair: every little step you take makes a difference, and the better you understand your enemy, the better position you are in to fight back.

Mythbuster

There is nothing you can do about your anxiety levels – they are fixed by your personality.
There is a grain of truth in this commonly held belief. Some people – due to their personality or lifestyle – are more prone to anxiety. But by understanding anxiety better, it *is* possible to control it!

1

Anxiety – friend or foe?

As we prepare to fight back against anxiety, there is one important question we need to answer straight away. In order to understand how anxiety is designed to work, we need to look at what it's there for in the first place. It's easy to think that emotions are just a nuisance, but in fact they are essential to the normal functioning of our brain. Anxiety is no different – so let's think about what it does.

Over to you!

Everyone's experience of anxiety is different, and throughout this book you'll see sections like this which ask you to think about exactly how some things feel for *you*. This will help you to apply the theory that you've read to your own situation. So wherever you see an "Over to you!" box, grab a notebook and take some time to jot down answers to the questions.

Let's start by thinking about a recent time when you felt anxious. Can you remember where you were, what it felt like, and what you did? Now ask yourself this question: What was it about how you were feeling in that moment that makes you so sure you were feeling anxious?

To help you think this through, note down some of the things you remember thinking, feeling, or doing. So...

- Where were you/what were you doing?
- What did you feel? (Include emotions and any physical sensations you remember.)
- Do you remember any of the thoughts that were running through your head?

The three main functions of anxiety

Everyone's experience of anxiety is different, but if we asked a group of people to do the same task, some common themes would emerge – experiences that we all have in common in those moments when we feel what we call "anxiety". Research investigating emotions has found three main functions of anxiety – certain jobs it seems to do within the brain. These are closely related to the way we experience it. Let's think about what those functions are – and how they relate to the way anxiety *feels*.

1 First and most important, anxiety is your brain's way of grabbing your attention.

This is one reason why usually people find it pretty easy to think of times when they were anxious. The way you feel grabs your attention and makes you aware that it is happening. Anxiety triggers physical changes in your body which you very quickly notice. All those classic "symptoms" of anxiety – butterflies in the stomach, sweating, feeling breathless – are signs that your brain is using your body to try to get your attention!

Common signs and symptoms of anxiety

- Heart beating faster
- Feeling more aware of your heartbeat or experiencing palpitations
- Trembling or shaking
- Fast/shallow breathing
- Feeling sick/butterflies in stomach
- Needing to go to the loo more than usual
- Indigestion/stomach cramps
- Sweating/hot flushes
- Headaches
- Difficulty concentrating or sitting still
- Trouble sleeping
- Feeling lightheaded/faint
- Heightened awareness of sounds/things going on around you
- Irritability
- Obsessive (round and round) thinking
- Inability to think clearly or logically

Anxiety's main job is to grab your attention when a part of your brain notices something that *might be*

significant. In particular, anxiety is usually triggered if it looks as if something important to you is threatened. There is a part of your brain constantly keeping track of what is going on in your life and the world around you. It lines up this information with the goals and rules that you also have stored in your brain.

Some of these goals are basic and shared by all of us – like "staying alive". Others are more complex and related to aspects of your own life or lessons you have learned in the past. So goals might be something like "I need to write a report that really impresses my boss" or important pieces of information such as "Last time I skied I fell over and hurt my knee really badly". The next time your brain flags up that something about your circumstances is related to a goal, rule, or previous experience you have stored, it needs some way to alert you – and what it uses is the combination of sensations we call anxiety.

> Anxiety is triggered when something going on around us threatens in some way a goal or rule, or reminds us of a previous experience which had a significant outcome.

So, let's say you have planned to go out after work tonight. Then, just as you are about to leave, you remember that a report you haven't finished has to be done by 9 o'clock tomorrow morning. You could run something off quickly before you go, but suddenly you feel a pang of anxiety. Why? Your brain is triggering anxiety to alert you that you have a goal to write a really impressive report, and your circumstances right now are threatening the successful achievement of that goal.

Let's think about another example. Have you ever put the wrong fuel in your car? For most people, putting fuel in their car is one of those "automatic pilot" things they do without really thinking. But a friend of mine recently did this with a hire car… and suddenly realized to her horror she was putting unleaded petrol in a diesel tank! But what was it that, halfway through filling the tank, made her realize her mistake? She described how she suddenly felt a pang of quite strong anxiety – her brain, working in her subconscious mind, had realized there was a clash between what she was doing and a subconscious goal (something like "I do not want to mess up this hire car and lose my deposit"!) and it triggered anxiety. This grabbed her attention, and the minute she focused on what she was doing she realized her mistake and was able to rectify it before it was too late.

Think about this situation. It is 3 a.m. and you are fast asleep. Then the phone rings! What do you feel? Most people admit they would feel a stab of anxiety. But why? You don't usually feel anxious when the phone rings. But because 3 a.m. is an unusual time to phone, most people make the link in their brains that something bad might have happened. This is a perfect example of how a worst case scenario suddenly starting to seem possible can trigger anxiety.

So anxiety is triggered when something going on around us threatens in some way a goal or rule, or reminds us of a previous experience which had a significant outcome. One other thing is always present with anxiety. It is what I call a Worst Case Scenario (WCS). This is the thing that you don't want to happen – the thing you are dreading and want to avoid. It could be failing an exam, being yelled at by your boss, having to do something you don't want to do, being attacked by a scary insect, animal, or reptile – each anxiety-provoking scenario has its own WCS. When your brain detects that the chances of this WCS being possible have just risen, it triggers anxiety to alert you.

Over to you!
What are your WCSs?

Think about the example you wrote about above, when you experienced anxiety. Can you identify what it was you were anxious about? What, in that example, was the worst case scenario? You might find it helps to think about the worst thing that could possibly have happened – and then write it down.

---

2 The second main role of anxiety is that it makes you ready to (re)act.

When you feel anxious, your brain activates a complex network of nerves, hormones, and other chemicals called the sympathetic nervous system. This system controls how ready you are to react to something –

when it is turned up, you are primed for action. It controls the well-known *fight or flight* response. When the sympathetic nervous system is activated, a chain of events occurs in your body preparing it for physical activity – fighting or, in the case of anxiety, running away! These events include the following:

- The release of hormones (including adrenaline) increases your heart rate and dilates (widens) the blood vessels which supply your heart and main muscles.

- Your heart beats faster, delivering more blood around the body.

- The blood vessels supplying everyday functions (such as digestion) narrow, so your blood is immediately diverted to the muscles, where it might be needed if you have to jump into action.

- Glucose is released into your blood and your breathing rate increases so that your blood becomes rich with the energy-giving sugar and oxygen you need to be able to move fast.

Anxiety also triggers changes within your brain. These too make you ready to react to the slightest hint of danger or risk. You might notice yourself feeling more alert and more likely to react to small things – noises or movements, for example.

Over to you!
How can you tell when you are "primed to react"?
Think about your example of an anxious episode. Do you remember
feeling more alert then? Were there sounds or movements you
responded to that you wouldn't usually respond to? Did you feel more
jumpy than usual or find it hard to sit still? What were the signs that you
were "primed to react"?

3 Finally, anxiety affects the way you are thinking.
Your brain doesn't just trigger changes to your physical
and emotional state. At the same time the alert it sends
pushes into overdrive the part of your brain that does
the analysing. The purpose of this is to give you the
chance to work out if you need to react, and, if so, what
that reaction should be.

Often it feels as if this is actually the *first* thing you
do when you are anxious, not the last! People often say
that it is because they are thinking certain things – "Oh
no, I hope I get this done in time" or "I really hope she
didn't hear me say that" – that the anxiety is triggered
in the first place. In fact, the reality is that your change
in thinking is actually something that happens later
on in your anxiety response. In moments of real life-
threatening danger, your brain can by-pass this stage
and trigger a physical reaction before you have even
had time to think. Before you even realize what you
are doing you have jumped out of the way of the car

that was about to hit you, or run away from the wasp buzzing near you, and only after you have reacted do you have time to think. We'll look later at the thought patterns that can be triggered by anxiety – and how they can be significant in anxiety problems.

Reminder: the three main roles of anxiety

- Anxiety warns you that something significant might be happening/about to happen.
- Anxiety primes you to react.
- Anxiety triggers your thinking so you analyse what is going on.

Mythbuster

Some people are not scared of anything.
No one is able to function normally without experiencing anxiety; it is a vital part of being alive. Anxiety helps you achieve your goals and avoid disaster, whether in your work, relationships or personal life.

2

When anxiety goes bad

Now that we understand the important role that anxiety has in the way our brains *normally* function, we can look at what exactly is going on when anxiety starts to cause problems. Anxiety is designed to protect us from harm, but it can and often does actually *cause* harm when it makes us react in ways that are unhelpful. We've looked at the three main functions of anxiety. Now let's look at the three most common ways anxiety can cause problems.

Mythbuster

Anxiety is a "bad" emotion. You should aim never to feel anxious again.

That simply isn't possible – anxiety is one of a set of emotions that are essential for the way our brains work.

The key is to learn how, why, and when anxiety can be so problematic – and how to avoid these common pitfalls.

1 Anxiety that is triggered too often, or inappropriately

As we have learned, exactly when anxiety is triggered is determined by the goals, beliefs, and plans we have. Some of these are things we all share, such as the goal to stay alive or protect those we care about. But we all also have a whole set of goals and beliefs about the world which stem from our experiences growing up, are features of our personality, or are just part of who we are. Growing through childhood and adolescence, we all learn some basic rules about how the world works and how we need to operate within the world to be successful. These experiences form the rules and beliefs we live by.

For most of us, then, these rules are accurate and helpful, so experiences such as "If I am nasty to someone, they probably won't like me" lead to us forming goals such as "I should always try to be nice to people if I want them to like me". These are the kinds of beliefs and rules that are helpful in successful adult life. Imagine, however, what happens if your childhood leaves you with some experiences that are harder to make sense of – say, an abusive and unpredictable parent. Imagine a child who tries their best never ever to get anything wrong so that their parent will not yell at them. This child might grow up with a rule that says "I must never ever make a mistake" because their experience is that making mistakes has very unpleasant consequences. Imagine what happens to that child when they grow up, trying to live life without *ever* making *any* mistakes. What they will find is that each time they are in a situation where they have – or even just might be at risk of making a mistake – their brain will trigger anxiety.

Sometimes our past experiences have led us to set rules or goals that simply are not possible. So we might push ourselves incredibly hard to achieve highly in everything we do, or try to juggle lots of different responsibilities without ever making a bad decision in any of them, or we might aim never ever to lose our temper with someone we are caring for. In all these cases the problem is that our goal/rule is just not possible for a normal human person! We are normal people trying to live to super-person rules! When this happens we are setting ourselves up for lots of anxiety.

> Problems can occur if you are trying to live your life according to rules or goals that are just not possible for a normal human person! If you are trying to live to super-person rules, you are setting yourself up for a lot of anxiety.

Echo Emotions
Remember I said that anxiety can be triggered when something about what is going on *now* reminds you of

something significant that happened in the past? Echo emotions are triggered in exactly this circumstance: when something happening in the present mirrors part of something that happened in that time long ago. If the original experience was traumatic, your brain is very hypersensitive to signs that it might be happening again – even a similar sound, smell, or noise can trigger it. Your brain triggers a very powerful emotion in response to what is happening, often totally out of proportion to what is happening now. It is reacting to what happened in the *past* rather than what is actually happening in the present, and these "flashbacks" can be very frightening and debilitating. These emotions – often accompanied by flashes of memories – can become very problematic and are strongly linked with something called post-traumatic stress disorder.

> Echo emotions occur when something in the present mirrors in some way something that happened in the past, and your brain triggers an emotion to warn you. The emotional intensity is matched to what happened in the past, so may be totally out of proportion to what is happening now.
>
> Post-traumatic stress disorder is an anxiety disorder which develops after someone experiences or witnesses a traumatic event. Sufferers experience memory flashbacks (triggered by sights, sounds, or thoughts which remind them of what happened),

physical symptoms of anxiety, and difficult emotional reactions which persist for many months (and even years) after the original event.

Phobias

Finally, there is, of course, one much more common example of inappropriate emotions. These occur when an intense fear is attached to something that isn't really threatening – phobias. Although some phobias develop because of a traumatic experience – and so are a kind of echo emotion – some have no logical cause whatsoever. Thousands of people are terrified of snakes even though they have never ever seen one! Other people find that they have developed a phobia of something entirely harmless, such as buttons or birds. In fact, phobias can develop about almost anything and are often illogical; we'll look at how these develop in more detail in Chapter 4.

2 Anxiety bonfires

The second way that anxiety can become a problem is when something is happening in your brain to make the anxiety *grow*. The way your emotions are designed to work is a bit like striking a match. The flame lights up, burns for a short time while it is needed, then dies out. Something significant happens and anxiety is triggered like that burst of flame. Your attention is grabbed, you analyse what is going on, and take any action you need to. The anxiety then dies out, as quickly as it erupted.

But, more often, what we experience doesn't feel like a small flame. Anxiety can last for a long time or even smoulder in the background with no apparent trigger. It can grow very quickly and feel totally out of control. Here we are dealing not with sparks of anxiety, but with great big anxiety bonfires.

Remember that one of the functions of anxiety is to trigger your thinking so you can analyse what is going on. Anxiety bonfires happen when we have become prone to thinking in certain ways which, instead of being constructive and helping us to analyse the situation that triggered the anxiety in the first place, actually make the anxiety worse. These unhelpful patterns of thinking are a bit like leaving balls of paper lying around in our brains. Then, when the match of anxiety is struck, instead of just burning out, it sets fire to this enormous pile of kindling. Here's an example of how this might happen in real life.

Dave is a postman. He loves his job and feels he is pretty good at it. He's never really made a mistake and he works hard to sort the mail and get it to the right houses when he delivers. There are two roads on his round with similar names and a business in one of the roads gets really cross if its mail gets lost. But that doesn't really bother Dave – he's pretty confident that he gets it right most of the time.

Phil is also a postman. But, unlike Dave, he doesn't really like the job. He's only doing it because he lost a job he

loved somewhere else. He finds it hard and often wishes he was back at his old job which he thinks he was much better at. He worries a lot that he might make a mistake because he is not concentrating. In fact, there are two roads he delivers to with similar names, and the other week there was a complaint from someone working at a business on one of the roads who reckoned he hadn't received a really important letter. Phil cannot get rid of the worry that it was his mistake. It's just the kind of thing he would do, and he's pretty sure that if he hasn't already got something wrong, he soon will.

Which of these two postmen do you think is more likely to struggle with anxiety? We don't know which is really better at the job, but we can predict clearly who will find anxiety a problem. This is because Phil's thinking – and his beliefs about himself – means that when anxiety is triggered, his worries will build it up into big fires. His head is full of kindling, and he may find anxiety smouldering away even when there isn't actually anything he needs to be anxious about.

Anxiety bonfires happen when we have become prone to thinking in certain ways which, instead of being constructive and helping us to analyse the situation that triggered the anxiety in the first place, actually make the anxiety worse. These unhelpful patterns of thinking are a bit like leaving balls of paper lying around in our brains. Then, when the

> match of anxiety is struck, instead of just burning out, it sets fire to this enormous pile of kindling.

Most of us, if we're honest, would admit that we have times when we're prone to this kind of emotional fire. We're all more likely to have negative patterns of thinking when we are tired or stressed out, but sometimes this becomes more than just an occasional nuisance. Some people find that they are caught in cycles of negative thinking, and this fuels anxiety fires so that they never really get any break. Their brain is constantly on the go, flitting from one worry to another. Some negative thoughts (we'll look at some common kinds of unhelpful thinking in Chapter 6) can trigger new sparks of anxiety, all of which add to the blaze going on inside your head. It can be very difficult to link the anxiety with any clear cause, and sometimes this means that life starts to feel very overwhelming and frightening. Anxiety blazes can also quickly take over your life.

3 The panic cycle

The third common way in which anxiety can start to create problems is really caused by one main feature of the way we experience anxiety – and that is just how strong the physical sensations it triggers can be. All emotions change the way we feel in some way, but anxiety in particular can cause sensations that are at best uncomfortable and at worst can produce real physical complications or feel pretty alarming.

The real risk with anxiety is one of two things. Some people become so scared of the physical consequences of anxiety that the minute they experience a spark of anxiety, and feel the sensations coming on, that in itself triggers several more sparks of fear. Of course, that makes their symptoms even stronger, which triggers more fear. You can see how this can quickly become a vicious cycle (see Figure 2.1). One man who was struggling with anxiety-related headaches explained it like this: "The trouble is that I know these headaches are so linked up to what I am thinking about them. If I don't keep myself distracted, I find myself worrying about whether I might get a headache. That worry then brings on the start of one, which makes me worry even more, which makes the headache worse. Sometimes I think the only way to get rid of the headaches would be to take out the bit of my memory which knows I get them!"

Figure 2.1: The panic cycle

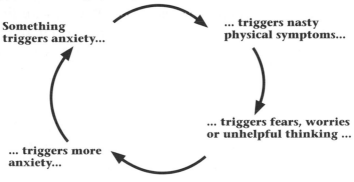

Something triggers anxiety...

... triggers nasty physical symptoms...

... triggers fears, worries or unhelpful thinking ...

... triggers more anxiety...

Panic attacks

Sometimes this cycle of symptoms feeding anxiety, which then feeds the physical sensations even more, can build up and up, meaning that symptoms become genuinely alarming. This can lead to what is called a panic attack.

> A panic attack is an attack of intense fear or anxiety that comes on very suddenly. Physical symptoms usually dominate, and sufferers often fear they are having a heart attack.

During a panic attack, the hormonal changes triggered by anxiety cause the heart to beat faster and faster. A person also becomes more anxious, their breathing rate changes, and they take shorter, shallower breaths. This means that the levels of oxygen and carbon dioxide in their blood change slightly, triggering unusual physical sensations such as tingling in the fingers and feeling faint. Tension in the muscles can lead to pains (including chest pain), and as the digestive system shuts down, some people feel sick or get stomach cramps or diarrhoea. As if all this wasn't bad enough, often people understandably become terrified that their symptoms are caused by something more serious – or will trigger something more serious, such as a heart attack. A panic attack can look very dramatic, and it is not unusual for people to find themselves in hospital as passers-by or worried family call for emergency help.

Fascinating fact

Breathing into a paper bag really can help calm a panic attack! This is because re-breathing the air you have just breathed out stops you from losing so much carbon dioxide and so lessens the strange symptoms that low CO_2 can cause. Often this helps people to start to feel calmer, because they realize that things are not as out of control as they had thought. However, any relaxation exercise or just thinking calmer thoughts and taking slower, deep breaths will also help – and might be easier than rushing round looking for a paper bag.

Physically, panic attacks are usually harmless, although you should always see a doctor if you have never experienced one before, just to put your mind at rest and make sure there is nothing else more serious going on. The real risk with panic attacks is the impact they can have on your life. If you have experienced a panic attack, it is very difficult the next time you are in similar circumstances, or feel the anxiety sparks, not to become afraid that the same thing will happen again. And, of course, that fear can itself then trigger a panic attack... and you're into the same cycle again. If you are caught in the panic cycle, it's very important to break the pattern – ideally before it gets too powerful. But remember, no matter how scary those symptoms feel, you can control them – and they are not as bad as they feel.

Over to you!

The risk with anxiety is not so much about what it might do to you but rather about what you might do or not do as a result. So how has your anxiety affected you? Are there things you don't do now because of your anxiety? Has it ever stopped you from taking an opportunity or prevented you from being able to do something you really wanted to do?

Here are some more questions to help you to think about the impact anxiety has on you:

- What would your friends and family say if they were asked what impact your anxiety has on you?
- If you had a magic wand and could change anything in the world that is currently affected by your anxiety, what would it be?

3

When what we do makes things worse
Part 1: Ignoring or trying to avoid anxiety

So far we have looked at what anxiety is designed to do when it works properly, and also at some of the ways in which anxiety can become a problem. But we need to understand two more very important things that can make anxiety grow and start to burn out of control. They are both about *the way we respond to anxiety* – things we do because we think they help, but which actually make things worse.

> Watch what you do! The way you respond to anxiety can be a significant part of developing an anxiety problem...

Anxiety is designed to be an aversive emotion – that is, it is designed to be unpleasant and to be really effective at grabbing our attention. No matter what feelings and sensations you wrote down in Chapter 1 when you were thinking about what anxiety feels like, the chances are they were things you did not find very pleasant to experience. Anxiety is a very physical emotion and we are hard-wired to try to avoid it where possible. But this can lead us to respond in ways which are unhelpful.

Trying to ignore anxiety

Perhaps the most common thing we do is try to ignore anxiety, or to push it down and suppress it in the hope it will go away. It's something we often do with feelings we don't understand or are not sure what to do about. Sometimes it can work: distracting ourselves from some feelings can help to lift our mood and change our perspective. But the trouble with anxiety is that its main job is to *make* us pay attention to something. Think of it like a small child who wants you to listen to them. What happens if we ignore a small child and hope they will go away? Do they? No, they get louder, more obvious, and more annoying until we do pay them some attention! Anxiety is very similar. Suppressed anxiety does not just evaporate – it smoulders beneath the surface. And, like a big fire that has not been put out properly, anxiety can re-ignite without warning. Often this happens at times when we are vulnerable – when we are tired, alone, or stressed out. Smouldering anxiety is very difficult to deal with because it is so far removed from what originally caused it, and it feels very uncontrollable and irrational. It can result in a constant low-level feeling of anxiety – what is called "free floating" anxiety – and this is very unpleasant.

Mythbuster

Anxiety is just a sign of weakness. You should just ignore it and get on with it.

Not true! Anxiety is there for a reason. Just ignoring it will not make it go away. If you experience anxiety, you need to get to the root of what is triggering it and why it has become such a big problem.

Avoiding things or running away

The second way in which our own actions make anxiety worse is when we start to avoid the thing or things that scare us. This is an important part of understanding how anxiety grows!

Think about this example. A young child has a bad experience when a neighbour's dog jumps up at them and barks in their face. This is a pretty scary thing to happen to anyone but particularly when the dog is as big as you

are. Next time that child sees the neighbour's dog how do you think the child will react? Probably by running away from the dog, or crying, or hiding from it. They would probably cross the road rather than risk walking past the dog on the pavement.

In the last chapter, we looked at the three ways in which anxiety can grow and become difficult to handle. Repeated triggers for anxiety; thinking and worries that build up small sparks into big fires; the terror of what will happen physically if anxiety gets the better of you and the physical consequences of all that emotion – all this can build up very fast. And our brains are very good at storing and remembering episodes of feeling very anxious – often without any particular relation to what actually happened in the end. In fact, anxiety can cause what is almost like a physical link between the part of our brain that logs the detail of that *experience* – where we were, what we were doing, how we were feeling – and the part of our brain that stores the memory of what happened as a result.

> Anxiety is designed to be an aversive emotion – that is, it is designed to be unpleasant and to be really effective at grabbing our attention.

Fear of something you have experienced
So how does this work in practice and how does it influence our reaction? Let's say that you are unlucky enough to have a bad experience in an exam when

anxiety just becomes so overwhelming that something happens – you run out, or throw up, or just make a real hash of the exam. The next time you try to take an exam, your brain will immediately link that situation to the memory of what happened last time. It's almost as if the minute you go into that situation that bit of your memory lights up and starts flashing and beeping a warning sound. Everything in your brain is telling you to get out of that situation, to stop the same thing from happening again.

So it's pretty understandable why, for most of us, our first reaction to something we found scary is to avoid it the next time. Many children have played with a wonderful balloon, then jumped on it and burst it. The loud noise and sudden disappearance of a loved toy are pretty traumatic if you are only eighteen months old! It's not at all uncommon, the next time they are offered a balloon, for children to react with fear, and, more significantly, to try to hide away – burying their head in their parent – or to push or throw the balloon away (as well as make a lot of noise to express their discomfort with the situation). If we have an encounter with something and it scares the life out of us, most of us will try to avoid it next time. This is particularly true if the last time was especially traumatic, either because something bad did happen or just because it *felt* really bad.

Fear of something you have not personally experienced
Sometimes you don't even have to have had the experience yourself to find your instincts telling you to avoid something. How many of us, in the days, weeks, months, and even years after 9/11, had to take a plane and struggled with suddenly feeling really anxious about it? One man I spoke to put it perfectly: "It's something I have done every week for years – I travel a lot by plane and usually I do it without a second thought. But after 9/11 I found myself feeling really anxious. I often sleep badly the night before a flight and I feel very uneasy throughout the process of checking in. I'm really edgy and I watch my fellow passengers really carefully. Even when I am on the flight I just cannot relax. It's as if every bit of me is telling me that the worst might happen."

A lot of common phobias are related to situations where, very occasionally, horrendous accidents or tragedies do happen. These are usually given a lot of attention in the media and really stick in the mind. Flying makes a lot of people very nervous, in spite of being one of the safest ways to travel – statistically, driving is *much* riskier, but we do that every day without a second thought! Your brain links that circumstance with a bad outcome – even though it did not happen to you – and therefore if you are in that situation, or even think about it, your brain automatically "lights up" the area storing the information about the worst case scenario, leading to an anxiety response. This may well make you less keen to fly (or whatever it is that is making you anxious) – so you start to avoid the thing which seems to trigger the anxiety.

Why avoiding things doesn't work
The problem with avoiding the thing that scares us is that we *think* avoidance controls our fear. By avoiding the scary thing we don't feel scared, therefore our anxiety is controlled. It's an instinctive response and in some situations it is a good plan – when avoiding angry lions, for example. But what if you just had a bad experience? What if it was just bad luck or a one-off thing? So the girl who threw up in an exam did so because she had a tummy bug, the guy who had the terrible car crash was just in the wrong place at the wrong time, and, in fact, aeroplane crashes are *really* rare. When we start to avoid the thing we are scared of, we have slipped into the trap of believing that we can control the chances of that bad thing happening again, because we are avoiding the situation we believe to be risky. The problem is that the natural conclusion of this belief is that if we *don't* avoid whatever it is, *the bad thing almost definitely will happen again*. The only thing stopping that from happening is our avoiding it.

Think of anxiety as a smoke alarm. Anxiety is triggered to warn you that something needs checking out because it *might* be important. Your brain warns you that something going on around you *might* threaten a goal, not that the goal is *definitely* threatened. One of the roles of anxiety is to trigger your analysing powers to identify whether there really is a problem and whether you need to do anything. The anxiety is not a sign of definite doom; it is a warning that something *might* need attention – just like a smoke alarm. Think about it. How many times has your smoke alarm gone off? How many times was there really a fire? Just like with the smoke alarm, most of the time all we need to do is check things are OK, and then we can move on.

> Anxiety is like a smoke alarm. It warns us that something significant *might* be happening, so that we can check it out. It does not mean that there definitely is a fire.

4

When what we do makes things worse –
Part 2: How phobias develop

Now that we understand how avoiding the thing that makes us anxious can make anxiety worse, we can start to see how serious anxieties develop and grow. When we start to avoid something, what we have done is started to treat anxiety as if it *definitely* means there is a problem. It's a bit like assuming that every time the smoke alarm goes off, there definitely *is* a fire. Even though we know that fires are rare, we react as if there must be one each time the alarm goes off.

This strengthens the link in our brains between what we are avoiding and that bad thing we fear. So, the child who had the bad experience with the dog feels anxious when she sees a dog because her brain links seeing dogs to that traumatic experience she once had – to the worst case scenario that the dog will jump up and bark at her. But then, as soon as she starts to avoid dogs, she never has any experiences where she meets a dog and it *doesn't* jump up at her, strengthening her belief that dogs will *always* jump up and the only way she can control the situation is to avoid them. This means that the next time she turns a corner and suddenly there is a dog, her fear is much stronger – she *must* avoid dogs, because if she doesn't, the thing she dreads will almost definitely happen!

Figure 4.1: How phobias develop

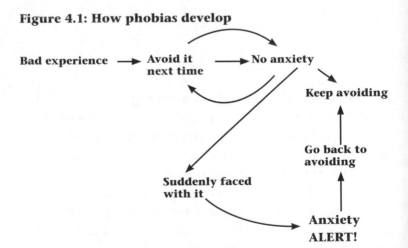

What I am describing here is the classic development of a phobia (see Figure 4.1). Phobias are extreme anxiety reactions to something specific, and they develop just like this. There may or may not have been some kind of traumatic initial experience. But it is the decision to try to avoid the thing triggering the fear that actually makes the anxiety grow, and from that point the chances are that that anxiety will continue to increase.

Anxiety spreads

Imagine that you are unlucky enough to get stuck in a lift one day. Not unexpectedly, you find yourself feeling quite anxious the next few times you have to go in lifts. So, to avoid feeling that fear, you start to avoid lifts. After all, there are usually stairs too, and you might even think about the health benefits of taking the stairs instead and see it as a good thing. But over time, as you keep avoiding lifts, your fear of them grows. Each time you get in a lift, you feel certain that you are going to get stuck. Panicked thoughts fill your mind, your heart races, and you feel yourself sweating throughout the journey and in those endless moments between the lift stopping and the doors finally opening. Eventually you find yourself unable to stay in a lift for more than one or two stops, and you often find yourself seized with panic and running out. It's not long before you become almost unable to go in lifts at all. Life is planned around avoiding lifts: using car parks that have stairs, not staying in big hotels, and always finding the emergency stairs anywhere you go.

Not only does anxiety grow, but once you start avoiding things it also spreads. The story above is actually one from my own life – it's something that happened to me after I was stuck in a lift as a child. By the time I started medical school as an eighteen-year-old, I could barely go in lifts at all. This was pretty tricky – especially working in a busy, six-floor hospital (I got pretty fit!), but, in fact, the worst thing about my phobia was that I could see it starting to spread. I began to feel scared in other situations that reminded me of that aspect of going in a lift that I hated the most: not being able to escape and feeling trapped. I started to dread flying (I hated that moment when the doors closed), going on the underground (looking out of the window and just seeing black), and I even found it hard to sit in the middle of a row at the cinema (how could I get out if I needed to?). I could see the anxiety starting to take over my life if I didn't do something about it.

Anxiety is like a forest fire: it does not stay still. Once you start running away from it, it grows and spreads. It is all too easy to end up penned into a corner, with lists of things you are avoiding as you desperately try to make the anxiety go away. Some people end up trapped in their homes, paralysed with anxiety.

> Did you ever play that game as a child where someone chased you up the stairs? Somehow, even though you knew it was just a game, it still felt scary when they chased you! Everything can be scary when you are running away from it. The trick with anxiety is to turn round and face it. It is much less scary when you stare it in the face than when it is chasing you into a corner.

Luckily for me, by that time I could understand how my anxiety was growing. I was able to practise on myself and try to work through my own phobia. Slowly and step by step, I beat it. We'll look at how to go about this in Chapter 5. But it's very important to understand why avoiding things you are scared of can make things worse. It is very easy to let anxiety push you back into a corner. One minute you are in control, and the next, anxiety controls you.

Over to you!
What triggers your anxiety?

Think about the main things that trigger your anxiety. These might be certain situations at home, school/college or work, objects, places, or people. Write them down as a list.

Can you think of a recent specific example of each – a time when you encountered the thing that triggers your anxiety? Write down a short summary of each one.

When what we do makes things worse: Part 2 **43**

In each situation, think about what you did to help you to cope with your anxiety. Do you ever do anything to try to avoid the thing that triggers your anxiety?

What impact does avoiding things have on your anxiety? Have you changed your mind about that since reading this chapter?

5

The anxiety line

Now that we have a basic understanding of how anxiety works, and just how it can come to take over our life, we need to start to look at how we go about taking back control.

The first thing to say before we start is that this is not easy. That may sound like a depressing way to start, but it is important to be realistic. You probably feel pretty anxious about the prospect of starting to challenge your anxiety. You may have spent many years of your life avoiding things or running away from your anxiety, and we are going to start to turn things around – so don't worry if you find things hard and don't get the hang of them at first. You may well find that you need some support; don't be afraid to discuss the things contained in these chapters with a friend or someone close to you.

The good news is that anxiety is a bit like a very small dog with a very big bark – it sounds much worse than it actually is! Most of anxiety's strength is in the fact that it keeps us so scared that we never challenge it. Just as if you went through the gate and realized that the dog that sounded so terrifying was actually only two feet high, anxiety often starts to dwindle very quickly once you realize that you can be much more in control of it than you thought. So once you get started it may not be as difficult as you imagined.

Let's deal with one misconception right now, though: no matter how well you do at these exercises, you will never eradicate anxiety from your life. However, anxiety will not have the same power over you, because you will be able to get back to the way anxiety is *supposed* to work. The key to controlling anxiety well is to learn how not to fear it and how to view it for what it really is: a warning sign that should trigger you to check something out. Remember, the smoke alarm going off does *not* mean that there is a fire; it means there are some signs that *might* indicate a fire. Most of the time all you need to do is check it out and then press the reset button.

What does anxiety feel like for you?

In order to start to handle anxiety better, the first thing to do is become more aware of what anxiety is and what it feels like. Often people who struggle with anxiety have got into the habit of suppressing it and trying to

ignore it, because they don't know what to do with it. They only become aware of anxiety when it has already started to grow.

The best way of improving your anxiety awareness skills is to start to note down exactly what anxiety feels like for you at different levels. What are the signs and symptoms you can pick up to identify that you are at low levels of anxiety? How do these change as you start to get more and more anxious? Think of your anxiety level as a line that goes from zero to ten, where zero is when you have no anxiety at all and are totally chilled out, and ten is the most anxious you can ever imagine being without your head exploding. Can you think of times when you have experienced anxiety at different levels along the line?

Over to you!
Charting your own "anxiety line"

This exercise will help you to become more aware of your own anxiety line and exactly what different levels of anxiety feel like for you. Find a piece of paper and draw yourself a line, marking 0 at one end and 10 at the other, like the line below. Make sure your piece of paper is bigger than this one, though, as you'll want to write some notes on the line in a moment.

0   **10**

Now think of the last time you felt really anxious. Can you remember when that was? Think about what was going on. You may want to jot down some of the details.

Where on the line would you say that experience was? Can you give it a number, or perhaps mark it on the line you drew?

Now think about how you felt at the time. Think about how you felt physically. Were there certain thoughts running through your head? Note them down next to wherever on the line you felt this experience was.

Here's an example of one person's anxiety line, taken from someone we'll call Jane. Jane was struggling with generally high anxiety and often reported that she did not know where it had come from. Her anxiety often overwhelmed her and she had had to take a lot of time off work because of the stress it put her under.

Last time I felt anxious: *"I was late for a work meeting and stuck in traffic. Was really anxious about what would happen if I missed the meeting."*

Score/place on line: *"It was pretty high. I'd say eight."*

How did I feel at that time? *"I felt as if I was about to explode. Head was racing. I felt really on edge and I couldn't concentrate properly on the radio, which I had on to try to calm me down. I kept trying to think of something I could do to get out of the traffic. I just couldn't think of anything, but the thoughts kept on racing through my mind anyway. I also started thinking that I wished I didn't have this job. I thought about just running away* *and never going back again. Physically, I felt sick, I know that. I was really agitated, tapping the steering wheel, fidgeting. I even stalled the car because my foot slipped off the clutch. I could feel a really bad headache coming on – my head felt under pressure, like a band being tightened around my forehead. I was breathing faster too, and my heart was really thumping. Thankfully the traffic cleared just then because otherwise I think I'd have had a full blown panic attack."*

8 – Feel very anxious. Cannot concentrate. Thoughts racing and out of control. Thinking of wanting to escape and run away.

0 —————————————————— **X** —————— 10

Feel sick. Very fidgety. Heart thumping. Tension headache starts to come on.

How does that compare to your own anxiety line? Remember everyone is different – the whole point of this is for you to work out how anxiety feels for *you*. Once you know what one level of anxiety feels like, you need to try to fill in as many points on the line as you can. So, for most people, the first example they think of will be fairly high – probably over five. Can you think of any examples when you have felt a slightly lower level of anxiety? Jane goes on to add another mark on her line when she thinks about how she usually feels at work.

"I do like my job, but I find it quite stressful because my boss can be really grumpy and he gets very impatient. I am always scared I might have done something wrong, or that he won't like what I have done. When I am at work I usually feel a bit anxious. If nothing particular has happened to make it worse, I would say I always feel at about level three on the line. I don't feel as bad as I do when I am at eight, as in the other example, but I still feel a bit sick or as if my stomach is churning. I quite often get stomach cramps, which I think is the anxiety. I can concentrate OK, but I feel quite on edge and I am easily startled by things. And I'm not totally with it – if someone tells me a joke, say, I don't get it at first because I'm just not in a place to find things very funny. I feel very tense and often get headaches by the end of the day. Thought-wise, I think things like 'I hope I have done this right', or, 'I hope he doesn't get angry with me.' And when I hear his door open, I immediately feel a stab of panic even if he is just going out to a meeting or something."

3 – Feel on edge. Slight sicky feeling, stomach churning and often stomach cramps. Easily startled.

8 – Feel very anxious. Cannot concentrate. Thoughts racing and out of control. Thinking of wanting to escape and run away.

0 ——— X ——————— X ——— 10

Find it hard to smile or find things funny. Worried thoughts common.

Feel sick. Very fidgety. Heart thumping. Tension headache starts to come on

Charting lower levels of anxiety

The lower half of this line is usually the most difficult to fill in, because very often people have become so good at suppressing or ignoring their anxiety that they only notice it once it gets over level five. If you do that, it can feel as if anxiety throws you straight in at the deep end when it is very difficult to do anything to help yourself. People often try relaxation exercises or techniques designed to help them to calm down, and find that they simply don't work. But trying these things out for the first time when you are at level eight or nine is a bit like learning to dive and starting out on the highest board – you are bound to belly-flop! Instead, you need to practise on some of the lower levels and then slowly move up from there.

At first it may feel as if you simply don't go through those earlier levels, but if you practise becoming more aware of your background anxiety level, you will start to notice how your anxiety gradually grows. So by thinking of times when she felt lower levels of anxiety, Jane is starting to get an idea of what it feels like for her when she is in this zone. This means that the next time she feels that way again she is more likely to notice it – and more likely to be able to do something about her anxiety before it grows and becomes overwhelming.

Over to you!

What is the lowest level of anxiety you can remember being aware of? Can you think of any examples of level one or two? What does that feel like? Mark it on your chart if you can remember any examples. If not, then think about this throughout the next few weeks – you may find yourself noticing things you haven't noticed before!

Mythbuster

Anxiety is like an on/off switch – either you're anxious or you're not.
There are many levels of anxiety. Learning to identify the lower levels so that you can take action before it becomes overwhelming is a key step in overcoming anxiety.

Emotional hijack

There is another reason why learning to identify the earlier levels of anxiety is important. When we get really anxious, something called "emotional hijack"[1] can occur. This term describes what happens when our brain triggers high levels of emotions such as anxiety and anger. Because such strong emotions may indicate really urgent danger, our brain can bypass the thinking part of the cortex and trigger an immediate response. This means that when you are under extreme anxiety you will find it much more difficult to control how you react. Trying to do anything constructive at this point is very difficult. It is a bit like a point of no return – I call it the panic zone. Everyone is different,

1. This term was first used in a book by Daniel Goldman called *Emotional Intelligence*.

but it usually kicks in somewhere around eight or nine. Jane, in our example, admitted that she felt she was on the edge of a panic attack. It is really important that you learn to identify anxiety before it gets this far, so that you can do something to help yourself before you reach the panic zone.

> Emotional hijack happens in emergencies, or when the anxiety triggered is very strong, and your brain bypasses the analysis of what is going on and causes a reaction. So you run away before you think about whether this is what you really want to do.

Think of it as a river. Anxiety often starts as small streams – things that are going on around you and trigger low levels of anxiety. As it builds up, those streams join together and form a river. As more streams join it, the river becomes wider, faster, and deeper. You could cross one of those little streams without too much trouble, but if you tried to cross that river, you would risk being swept away. Sometimes anxiety keeps on building up until it leads to panic. This is a bit like your river going over a waterfall. You cannot paddle your way out of trouble when you are about to go over a waterfall – the current is much too strong. You need to start changing direction before it gets to this stage.

Over to you!

Where is your panic zone?

Looking at your anxiety line, is there a point on the line where you know that you start to act or think less rationally? Is there a point beyond which you would find it hard to do anything constructive or to think straight?

Over the next couple of weeks, keep working at filling your line in. Think about the questions raised in this chapter. Do you have a point of no return, or panic zone, and where on the line is it? At what level on the line do you usually notice that you are feeling anxious? Have there been times when you have experienced low-level anxiety and wouldn't have called it that, or even noticed it? Do you tend to suppress anxiety and only become aware of it when it is already quite high up the line? Can you start to practise being aware of lower levels of anxiety? It's worth also asking yourself at various times throughout the day: Where on the line am I now and what do I feel like? Practise recognizing your anxiety level, and add to the line if you become aware of more details.

6

A quick lesson in relaxation

By now you should be starting to feel more aware of your anxiety, and you might also be getting better at noticing times when you are feeling anxious. But what can you do in those moments to try to bring your anxiety levels down? If you know that you are starting to get carried away on a river of anxiety – that your anxiety level is going up and getting dangerously close to the panic zone – what do you do? Or if you are stuck with a smouldering low level of anxiety that you just cannot get rid of, how do you break free?

This section is about the antidote to anxiety – relaxation. If you imagine that every spark or flame of anxiety moves you further up the anxiety line towards ten, relaxation is what brings you back down towards zero. It is your anxiety fire extinguisher!

Of course, it isn't quite that simple. Throughout the course of a normal day, our levels of stress and anxiety go up and down naturally according to what we are doing. If your day has enough balance in it, you should remain roughly at the same level overall – somewhere near the zero end of the line. But if you are struggling with anxiety, it means there is an imbalance – too many things are pushing you up the line. Or you might find that a very anxiety-provoking situation suddenly pushes you right up to the top of the line. When that happens, a key part of managing anxiety is learning what you can do to bring things back to normal.

> Relaxation is your anxiety fire extinguisher.

What exactly *is* relaxation?

Relaxation is about much more than just controlling the thoughts and worries that fuel anxiety. It is about physically relaxing and bringing down the levels of the hormones and other chemicals that have flooded your body as part of the anxiety or stress response. Most people think that relaxation is something that comes naturally – to other people! Few of us find it easy, but we assume that other people do. Of course, the truth is that relaxation is difficult for everyone and it is often something we need to learn.

There are two key things to remember about relaxation. The first is that it is important to build relaxation into your daily life. This is particularly important if you live a very stressful life or push yourself very hard. Stress triggers the same physiological system as anxiety, so if your stress baseline is very high, you are much more likely to find anxiety being triggered. Regularly scheduling relaxing activities into your life helps to keep stress levels down.

> It is important to build relaxation into your daily life. This is particularly important if you live a very stressful life or push yourself very hard.

The second thing that is particularly important when tackling an anxiety problem is to find a way of relaxing and calming down *in the moment*. You need to become really practised at something you can do in that moment when you feel your anxiety level rising up the line, before you reach the panic zone. You need to know that it will be effective and to feel confident that it will help you keep control.

Mythbuster

Relaxation time is just another excuse to be lazy! Doing nothing is unproductive.
This really isn't true. Driving yourself hard all the time without ever relaxing is like driving a car without ever refilling it with petrol. Relaxation is

essential – and the busier you are, the more important it is.

Relaxation exercises are just one way of learning how to relax "in the moment". Their main value is that they relax both mind *and* body. Relaxation exercises selectively and deliberately overcome some of the changes that anxiety triggers in your body. They counteract the things that can build up and fuel panic attacks, and they work to take your body and brain off red alert. They are popular because they teach you how to relax in moments when your anxiety or stress levels are very high – the moments when relaxing is most difficult. However, for the same reason, they are actually quite hard to get the hang of and, for most people, take a lot of practice.

Relaxation exercises

There are lots of relaxation exercises and resources around (have a look in the *Useful resources* section at the back of this book for suggestions). For a very simple relaxation exercise, see the box below (pp. 60–62). But whichever exercise you choose, the golden rule is to start out using it when you are *already pretty chilled out.* This may seem odd, but you need to learn how to use the exercise before you try it out at a time when it will be really hard. It's like learning to drive: you start on quiet back roads, and only once you are more confident and know what you are doing do you tackle busy roads!

So start out practising your relaxation exercise when you are somewhere safe (usually at home) and comfortable, and will not be interrupted. Do it at a time when your anxiety levels are low and when you are not under too much pressure (so not ten minutes before you have to dash out to collect the kids from school). Remember that practice makes perfect. So when you have started to get the hang of your relaxation exercise, keep doing it! Every time you practise it you are strengthening your relaxation skills, and this means you will find it easier when you do try to use it in an anxious moment.

When you feel pretty confident going through the exercise at a low anxiety level (below three), try it out when you are feeling slightly higher levels of anxiety (not too high – say, between three and five). Still try to find a time when you can be in a safe, comfortable place – perhaps at the end of a stressful day or before you go out to do something that you know is making you anxious. Practise it then, and see how you get on. It may well take more practice to get the hang of bringing yourself down from that level of anxiety, so don't be disheartened!

Once you can use the exercise to calm yourself down (that is, it reliably brings you down the anxiety line) when you are at home, try it out elsewhere. Depending on the exercise you choose, you might need to adapt it in some way. Try to identify the key points in your relaxation exercise: how it calms your breathing, what changes it makes to your thinking, and how you take control of your physical sensations. Start by trying to use your skills to help you bring those anxiety levels down when you are somewhere you spend a lot of time, perhaps at work. As you get better and better at it, you can practise calming yourself down when you are out and about.

The key to mastering any relaxation exercise in order to help control anxiety is realizing that you *can* be in control. Once anxiety is triggered, you do *not* have to get pushed into the panic cycle we learned about in Chapter 2. Good luck – and keep practising. Remember, you can never be too relaxed!

> Here is a very quick relaxation exercise. It isn't complex or particularly clever, but it really does help to stop anxiety from growing and gives you a chance to take control back if you are on the verge of panic.

For this exercise you need to find a song or piece of music which you find calming. It may be something that has particularly calming words or reminds you of a safe place or someone special. It needs to be a piece of music you like, because you will be listening to it a lot! There may be more than one piece, but at first stick to two or three at the most. Put the music on and, if you can, set it to play several times. Find somewhere comfortable you can sit or lie down – somewhere you feel safe and are not going to be interrupted. At first it's best to practise the exercise when your anxiety levels are low, so choose whatever the best time of day is for you.

As the music plays, either hum the tune or, if you want to, sing the words. This part is very important because it forces you to regulate your breathing. Try to get to the ends of the phrases or lines each time – this will encourage you to take nice deep breaths. Repeat this several times as the track repeats.

Practise this exercise as often as you can – a couple of times each day would be great. Each time, try to be somewhere calm and quiet, and do what you can to avoid interruptions. The idea is that you will start to associate this song with being calm and safe. The more you practise the exercise, the stronger the association will be.

Once you have mastered the exercise, you can start to use it to help you to calm yourself and move back down the anxiety line. Start out by trying it one day when you feel your anxiety has risen, but not too far – perhaps up to around five. At this level you will feel some of the symptoms of anxiety but you should also feel fairly in control. Find somewhere where you can grab five minutes of peace, put your track on (you can carry it with you on an MP3 player), and go through the exercise a couple of times. Make sure you do the humming. If you might be overheard, then you can always hum in your head, but make sure you breathe as though you really are humming!

The more you practise this exercise, the more effective it will be. Eventually some people find that even if they do not have the music with them, humming the tune helps them to feel calmer and back in control. The beauty of this *exercise is that it is quick, easy, and very portable. You can play the tune while walking along if you are outside, hum it to yourself as you are travelling or working, and even listen to it quickly in the toilet if you need a few minutes to calm yourself!*

7

Clearing out the kindling

In Chapter 2 we looked at how certain patterns of thinking can make anxiety worse and build up the normal healthy sparks of anxiety into great big anxiety bonfires. This chapter is an introduction to starting to clear out those unhelpful styles of thinking.

Keeping a thought diary is the best way of becoming more aware of the thoughts running through your mind and how they are feeding or affecting your anxiety and other emotions. Don't worry if you don't get much written down at first – it takes practice and you will get better at it!

Over to you!
Making a thought diary
Before you can start to identify the thoughts that are providing kindling

for your anxiety bonfires, you need to monitor *all* your thinking in those moments when you are struggling with anxiety. To do this, keep a thought diary. Write in the diary each time you have an episode of anxiety. So, you might write in it each time your anxiety levels start to go up on the anxiety line you charted in Chapter 5.

Each time you write in the diary, note down each of these things:
- Where were you and what happened?
- What level of anxiety did it trigger? (Note the number on the anxiety line.)
- What did you feel (physically as well as emotionally)?
- What thoughts went through your mind?
- What did you do as a result of feeling this way? (This might help you to notice any situations where you avoid things that make you anxious, or when your actions make your anxiety worse – for example, if you fail to do something helpful or try to ignore/suppress anxiety.)

You'll need to devote a special notebook to this diary and to keep it for a good few weeks, so that you get enough examples to look through. Sometimes you might write in the moment you feel anxious. Other times – perhaps more usually – you might not be able to write then, either because you are too anxious (if you are in that panic zone) or because it just isn't practical. Try to write as soon as possible so that you don't forget the details.

Analysing your thinking
Once you have a good set of entries noted down in your thought diary, see if you recognize any of the

following common bits of thought-kindling in the things you have written down.

Negative styles of thinking

This is the typical negative mindset of the pessimist. These kindling thoughts are about focusing on anything negative that has happened and ignoring anything positive. They predict negative things in the future and play down any successes. They assume failure and catastrophe wherever possible. So you probably will mess that thing up you have to do tomorrow... the traffic probably will be bad... everything you said at tonight's dinner party was utterly stupid...

All or nothing thinking

Often called black and white thinking, this describes situations where you feel things are either one thing or the other, with no grey areas in between. It means that you either succeed absolutely – or fail totally; you cannot do well if you do not achieve the absolute best. People who think like this tend to set very high standards and do not allow for any margins when they – or other people – are working towards those aims. They may actively look for signs of failure, and then declare their work (or whatever it is) useless and feel totally dissatisfied with the outcome. So an evening might feel like a total disaster just because one person was unable to come at the last minute or because one small thing didn't go according to plan. This style of thinking can combine with catastrophizing (see below) to lead people to feel extremes of anxiety because they have a goal that things *must* go 100 per cent well – and how often do things really go 100 per cent perfectly?

Catastrophizing

Catastrophizing – or snowballing, as I prefer to call it – is something we are all prone to when we are under stress, anxious, or worried about something. It describes the way in which our mind can make great illogical jumps between something that has happened (or we fear may happen) and things that may or may not be true or happen in the future. So we might accidentally say the wrong thing to a colleague. This triggers thoughts such as, "Oh no, they will tell everyone I was horrible to them." This then leads us to start worrying: "Everyone will think I am a horrid person... no one will like me... no one will want to know me." Before we know it we are worrying about future things: "I will always be alone... I'll never get married... I'll die all alone!" Reading a typical thread of catastrophizing thoughts might seem almost comical, but in the moment it feels as bad as that last thought – as if something you did inadvertently, in this case a throw-away remark to a colleague, may have sealed your fate for life. Small mistakes lead you to worry and panic about dreadful worst case scenarios that in reality will probably not happen.

Personalization

This is an interesting kindling thought pattern because it is actually a very common tendency and it also has an obvious potentially positive side. Personalization is when you tend to take responsibility for things even if they are not really something you should be controlling. It means you are often someone others can – and do – rely on, but it also means you may feel very guilty about things that aren't your fault at all. So you might feel guilty because someone else struggles to make friends at a social event, or if something wasn't done, even if it wasn't your job to do it in the first place. Spot this thinking pattern by thoughts such as "I should have done that" or "I wish I had known she felt like that", or by constant feelings of guilt.

Negative mind-reading

This last common kindling pattern describes someone who is constantly worrying about what other people are thinking, because it is sure to be something negative. This kind of thinking tends to be more common in people who are not very confident and usually comes up in social situations. Look for thoughts such as "I bet they are laughing at me" or "Well, he obviously doesn't want to talk to me" or "She thinks I am a real idiot", when there isn't actually much evidence to support those thoughts.

As you read through your diary, note when you are showing signs of kindling thinking. You might want to highlight any thoughts you identify. How do they relate to your anxiety? Are there thoughts that come up again and again?

Sometimes a thought can give a clue to an underlying goal or rule you live by. So, for example, all or nothing thinking is very common in people who push themselves to achieve superhuman levels in everything they do. Ask yourself: Is there a rule underlying this? Do I put pressure on myself to always achieve highly? Why? The rules we live by are often automatic. We learn them in childhood and often never question them again. But our childhood perspective on life can be unreliable, particularly if difficult things are going on at the time, or if someone influential also imposes harsh or unrealistic standards. Ask yourself if anything from your past is triggering these unhelpful patterns of thinking.

Over to you!
Identifying frequent offenders

Most people find there are a few thoughts that come up again and again in their thought diaries. They might be beliefs about themselves or someone else ("I'm so useless to not be able to do this"), rules or goals that they force themselves to live by ("I must never ever make a mistake"), or one of the unhelpful thoughts listed above ("This is my own stupid fault"). It is helpful to identify these frequent offenders, so why not list them in your diary?

Challenging common kindling thoughts

The next step of course is to ask yourself how accurate these thoughts really are. Are they influenced by how you are feeling at the time? Are they thoughts other people would agree with, and does the evidence really agree with them? Remember, these thoughts greatly influence your feelings and emotions. Do you want to live your life by them? Do you really agree with them?

You might find it helpful to take each thought in turn and do some "for" and "against" analysis of it. What is the practical evidence supporting that thought? And what about evidence against? Don't forget to consider about what your friends or relatives would think or say.

Over to you!

Take some time to note down the evidence for and against a few of your common kindling thoughts. For each one, draw a line down the middle of a sheet of paper. Write "For" on one side and "Against" on the other. Then try to note down as much evidence in both columns as you can. When you've finished, put it to one side — but keep it to hand. You might find over the next few days that you think of more to note down.

Once you have challenged your thought(s), try to come up with a more realistic version of what you really believe. For example: "Right now it feels as if getting stuck with this phobia is all my own stupid fault. It is true that I have done some things that have not helped, and which have contributed to just how much it affects me. But the thing that started it off wasn't my fault – it was just bad luck – and I didn't realize that what I was doing was actually making things worse. Now I am taking control and making things different – and this is just the first step."

These thoughts will help you to counteract the kindling thoughts when they try to nag at you. Some people find it helpful to write out the "truth" version on a piece of card and keep it in their pocket, wallet, or bag. Then if the kindling thought does attack, they have their defence ready to draw.

Understanding, identifying, and challenging unhelpful thinking patterns like these (as well as some of those super-person goals or rules we sometimes live by, mentioned in Chapter 2) is the basis of a therapy called cognitive behavioural therapy (CBT). It's impossible for us to cover all aspects of CBT in this one chapter, but we can start to become more aware of some unhelpful thoughts and how they influence our anxiety levels. If you would like to go through a more complete course of CBT and get further support identifying and challenging unhelpful thoughts, there are some great free web-based resources that will do just that for you. Check them out (see the **Useful Resources** section at the back of this book) or talk to your doctor about a referral for CBT.

8
Starting to win back ground
Part 1: List your fears

This is the most practical step in fighting anxiety –
and it may well be one you are impatient to get on to,
especially if your anxiety is limiting or restricting what
you do. Remember, however, how important it is to
take your time getting here! The previous chapters are
an essential part of setting the foundations in order to
tackle this stage successfully.

Before you move on to this stage

- Make sure you are aware of your own anxiety levels and what they feel like. See Chapter 5.
- Have a method of relaxation well and truly practised and perfected so that you feel confident you can handle moderate levels of anxiety when triggered (levels below that all-important panic zone). See Chapter 6.
- Identify any common "kindling" thoughts which might strike when you try to challenge your anxiety, and have a "true" version ready for if things do get difficult. See Chapter 7.

This is the final step in fighting anxiety, and it's a tool to help you to start to win back some ground where you have become caught in a cycle of avoiding something – and are struggling with your anxiety as a result.

You will remember that when you have built up a phobic reaction to something, your brain has linked your being exposed to something with the WCS that you dread. Every time you have avoided whatever that something is, this link has been strengthened, as you have believed the WCS didn't happen only because you avoided the situation. What we need to do is help your brain to understand that the link it has made may not actually be accurate. We need to teach your brain that sometimes you can be exposed to that thing without anything bad happening.

Now, before you panic let me reassure you. I am not

about to suggest that you think of the most terrifying scenario possible and then go and expose yourself to it! No, quite the opposite. Remember the driving analogy? When you are learning to drive, you start on the easier roads first. It will be the same here. What you need to do is start right at the lowest level of the thing you have been avoiding and gradually work your way up.

Starting to challenge your fears

Let me explain this by going back to my own experience of developing a phobia of lifts. I had got to a stage where this was becoming a real nuisance in my life and was even interfering with my job in the hospital. So I knew I needed to overcome it. I made a list of all the scary lift-related situations I could think of. I brainstormed all kinds of lifts that I would ever potentially have to go in. I ended up with a list of different kinds of lift, but also things such as watching lifts or having other people take the lift while I took the stairs. These were a lot less scary but still actually made me feel anxious.

The next step was to put those things in order, with the scariest at the top and the least scary at the bottom. To do this I gave each a rating out of ten, where ten was the most terrifying thing ever and zero was not scary at all.

Have a go at doing this yourself. You might find it difficult to do on your own, so perhaps ask a friend to help. You might find the process of imagining all the most anxiety-provoking situations itself produces some anxiety, so take your time and try not to push yourself.

If you find it very difficult, then try to think of a couple of things for the list at a time, then take a break and do something that you find relaxing or comforting. Remember, it is not just about thinking of situations that you find utterly terrifying; actually, the aim is to think of some that are not nearly as bad!

Over to you!
Brainstorming your own list

Let's take a minute for you to do this for your own phobia. First of all, brainstorm a list of all the ways you might come into contact – in any way – with the thing you are scared of. So, if you are scared of spiders, you might include going into the spider house at the zoo, finding a spider in the bath at home, seeing a picture of a spider in a magazine...

If it is public places that you find scary, you might include going to the supermarket or the cinema, but also walking to the end of your road, or even maybe just standing outside your front door for a few minutes and watching people go by. Write your list down in your notebook.

The next thing to do is try to put them in order. Give each one a rating from zero to ten (ten is the scariest possible and zero is not scary at all). Write the list out again in order, from the least to the most scary.

How have you done? If you find that your list is full of things scoring five or more, then you need to try again another day and think of some less scary things. Perhaps ask a friend to help. You will need to have a good spread of examples on your list before you move on to the next chapter.

9

Starting to win back ground
Part 2: Your road to recovery

Once you have compiled a good list of the kinds of situation that might trigger your anxiety, you are ready to move on to the next stage: to draw what I call a road diagram. This is rather like thinking about a long journey. If you wanted to go from London to Edinburgh, you could draw yourself a diagram of all the places you would need to go past on that journey. You could even add smaller steps such as "Fill car with petrol". We want to draw a similar diagram for all the stages you will need to get past as you overcome your anxiety. You'll need a big piece of paper for this (A4 at least). Draw a long wiggly road on it, then write "Start" at one end and "Finish" at the other (see Figure 9.1).

Next, put each of the things on your list on to your road diagram. Some of them – the ones with higher scores – will be quite near the finish. At the moment they feel very scary. Others might be nearer the beginning. You can see an example for my own lift phobia in Figure 9.2.

Figure 9.1: Starting to work out your own road map

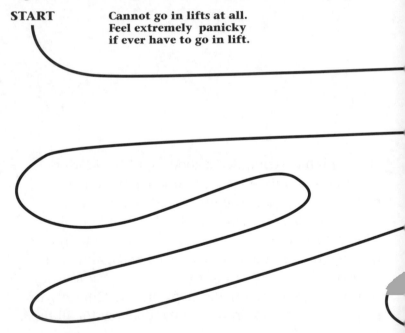

START

Cannot go in lifts at all.
Feel extremely panicky
if ever have to go in lift.

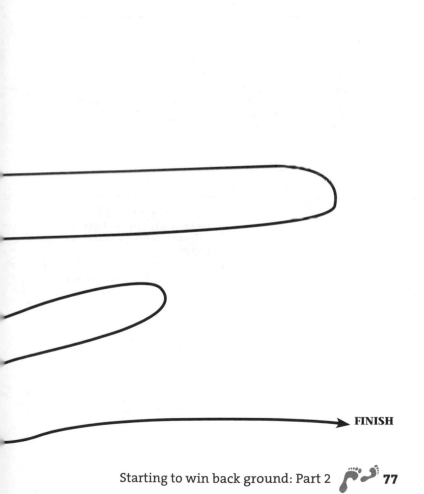

FINISH

Starting to win back ground: Part 2

Figure 9.2

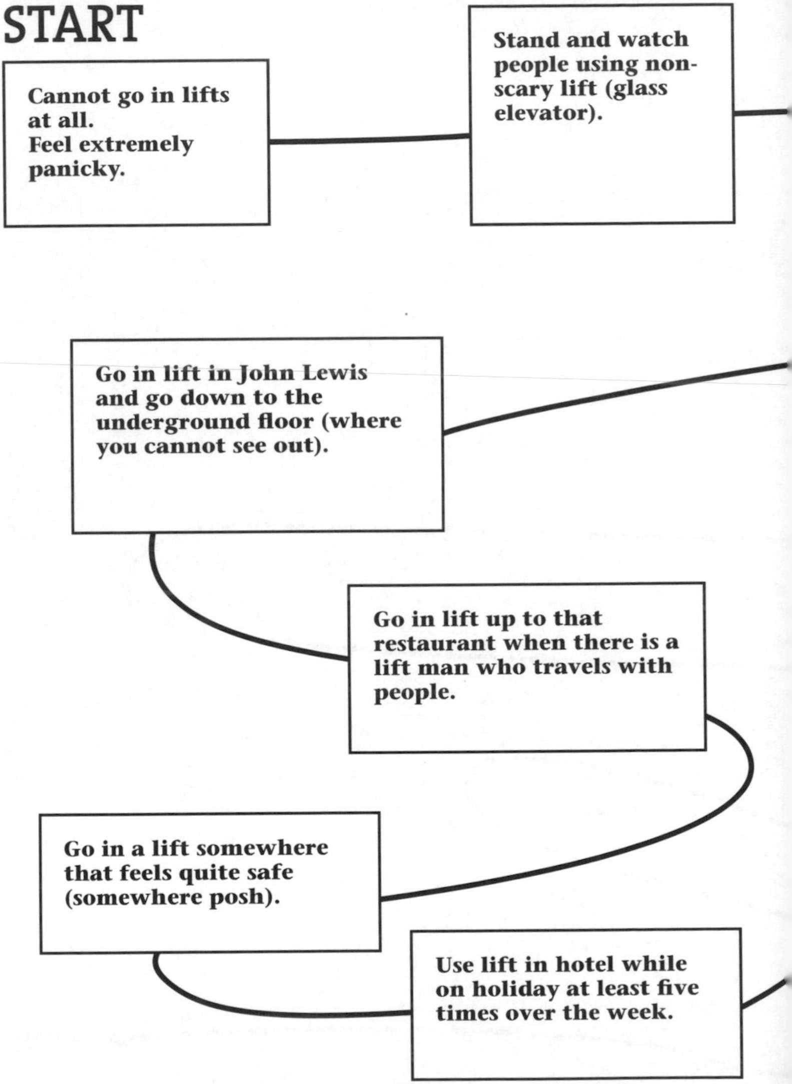

START

Cannot go in lifts at all.
Feel extremely panicky.

Stand and watch people using non-scary lift (glass elevator).

Go in lift in John Lewis and go down to the underground floor (where you cannot see out).

Go in lift up to that restaurant when there is a lift man who travels with people.

Go in a lift somewhere that feels quite safe (somewhere posh).

Use lift in hotel while on holiday at least five times over the week.

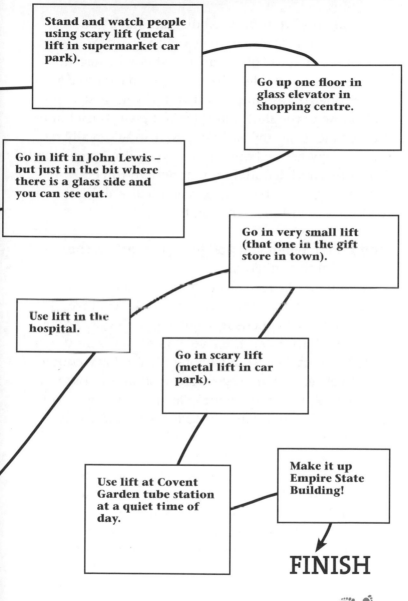

Stand and watch people using scary lift (metal lift in supermarket car park).

Go up one floor in glass elevator in shopping centre.

Go in lift in John Lewis – but just in the bit where there is a glass side and you can see out.

Go in very small lift (that one in the gift store in town).

Use lift in the hospital.

Go in scary lift (metal lift in car park).

Use lift at Covent Garden tube station at a quiet time of day.

Make it up Empire State Building!

FINISH

Make sure that your finished diagram has a good number of well-spaced markers on the road. You want to avoid having too big a gap anywhere because this indicates that you might be trying to take too big a step in one go. Also important is that your first step is quite close to the start point. Do not give yourself too big a challenge in the early stages. It should really be something you rated quite low in your list – preferably one or two and definitely no more than three.

What you want to do is move gradually along the road. Take your time – this isn't a race!

Step 1: Plan when you are going to start on the first all-important step

This shouldn't be too challenging so it should be quite easy to plan. When you go and do whatever it is, notice what happens to your anxiety levels. As you are there, think about the level you are on (zero to ten on the anxiety line from Chapter 5). You have chosen a relatively easy step, so your levels shouldn't rise too high, but do remember your relaxation exercise – you know what to do if you start to feel uncomfortably anxious. Whatever you do, don't let that spark of anxiety panic you – remember it is an empty threat trying to stop you from breaking free! Use your relaxation skills and challenge any kindling thoughts. It might be worth taking a friend who can help you to stay calm. Remember, you are in control. Do not be afraid of the anxiety – it is just your brain setting off the smoke alarm because that is what it has learned to do. There is nothing for you to fear, so remind yourself just how unlikely it is that your WCS will happen.

Step 2: Keep repeating this first step several times

Yes, I really did go and spend time watching people go into and out of lifts, and actually I did this more than once! I kept repeating that stage until my anxiety came down to almost nothing. And you will find the same: each time you repeat a stage on your chart it will provoke slightly less anxiety as your brain learns that you *can* in fact do this without the dreaded WCS happening. So the first time you might find yourself going up to level five or so, but the second time only three or four, and so on. When you can complete this level without it triggering anxiety, you are ready to think about moving on to the next destination.

Step 3: Think about moving on to the next step – but only when you are ready

Using this simple three-step rule, you can move along your road diagram stage by stage. Remember, some steps will be harder than others, so take your time and go easy on yourself. Don't push yourself too hard or make things more difficult – for example, by trying a new step when you are already stressed out. Celebrate each step you take forward and remember to move your marker on. Every move you make is a little bit more ground won from your anxiety. Put your diagram up somewhere where you can see it, and find a marker to indicate where you are on your journey (if you can stick it to the fridge, a magnet works well).

Don't forget to celebrate!

Moving along this diagram is a *huge* achievement, so give yourself plenty of credit. It's worth planning small treats and celebrations for each new step you achieve. You might also want to plan something special to mark the moment when you get to the end of your road diagram. It's a big achievement, so mark it well![1]

---

1. Yes, I did make it up the Empire State Building – eighty-six floors in forty-five seconds (apparently – it felt longer to me)! It wasn't the most fun trip of my life and I probably wouldn't choose to do it again, but I did it. And, much more important, it got me to a stage where most everyday lifts are manageable for me. Over the years (that was over a decade ago) lifts have simply become an everyday experience rather than something that fills me with fear. In fact, most lifts don't cause me any anxiety at all, although I must admit I still don't like those metal car park lifts very much and I absolutely never go in the lift at Covent Garden station in the rush hour!

10

Looking forward

This book has been a quick introduction guiding
you through some of the important steps in tackling
anxiety. It really is about the "first steps" out of anxiety,
so do get some more help if you need it, and don't be
afraid to talk to your doctor for more support.

I am passionate about helping people to work
through anxiety because I know the massive impact it
can have on your life, but I also know that things can
change magnificently with some good support to help
you fight back. Anxiety relies on the fact that people
never challenge it – they just keep running away. We
live in fear of something that usually doesn't happen.
How many times has your WCS actually happened?
How likely is it? What is much more real is the impact
that the fear of that WCS might have on your life. This

means that the thing you should be scared of is not the WCS but the fear it provokes; that is what can control and limit your life.

Fearing fear itself

One of my favourite quotations relating to anxiety comes from one of the Harry Potter books.[1] In this book Harry (the boy wizard) has been learning how to fight the Boggart. Boggarts are magical creatures which, when you face them, turn into the thing you fear most. For Harry, the Boggart turns into a Dementor and fills him with so much terror that at first he cannot fight at all but is totally paralysed with fear (you might say it pushes him straight into his own panic zone). Dementors are big black creatures in cloaks which J.K. Rowling based on her own experiences of anxiety and depression. When Dementors are around, they suck all the happiness out of you and make you feel as if you will never be happy again. You feel shaky and cold, both physically and emotionally. There is a conversation in the book in which Harry explains to his teacher what the Boggart turns into for him and how much this scares him. The teacher's reply amazes Harry because he expects to be laughed at for being a wimp. Instead, the teacher responds, "That suggests that what you fear most of all is – fear. Very wise, Harry."[1]

1. Rowling, J. K., *Harry Potter and the Prisoner of Azkaban*, London: Bloomsbury Publishing, 2004.

Remember as you fight your fear that it is often full of empty threats. I hope that this book has helped you to understand your anxiety better. If you are one of those people whose personality or experiences have left you more prone to anxiety than others, do not despair. It needn't control you. You do not have to become someone you are not in order to find a way through your anxiety. You can learn how to check things out and "reset" your anxiety. You can learn how to make that smoke alarm less sensitive.

Good luck in fighting back against your anxiety. Whatever happens, take pride in the fact that you are not giving in and letting it control you. It *is* possible to work through fears that have kept you imprisoned for years. So do allow yourself to look forward, not plagued by those kindling thoughts full of negative predictions and doom-laden prophecies. Dream of a future where anxiety does not control you. Then take the first steps to making that dream a reality.

For the family

Supporting someone who is struggling with anxiety can be very difficult. Anxieties often seem totally irrational from the outside, and you may find yourself very frustrated with the way their anxiety seems to affect them, and their apparent inability to fight back.

I hope you have found this book helpful, even though it is written as though speaking to sufferers themselves. Everyone experiences anxiety, so even if you do not struggle with it yourself, you may find some of the exercises help you to become more aware of what anxiety is and how it can affect people. You may be able to help the person you are supporting by working through some of the "Over to you!" exercises together, particularly in the more practical stages towards the end of the book.

How can you help?

There are three really important ways in which you can help someone who is struggling with anxiety:

Know your (and their) enemy

Anxiety wreaks its havoc because of the utter terror with which it fills people. However, most of the time these fears are never going to be realized. You can help by learning about how anxiety works – and about how the person you are supporting has got so trapped by its impact on them. Remember that the fear they feel is real, but the outcome they are dreading usually is not. Help them to understand how their fear is being triggered unnecessarily, and accompany them on their journey to challenge that fear.

Help them to use the fire extinguisher

The ultimate antidote to anxiety is relaxation. However, this is not an easy skill to learn, particularly if you are prone to anxiety. Remember that this is about ongoing relaxation – throughout the week – as well as finding exercises or rituals that help to calm the person you are supporting in the moments when anxiety strikes. Help them to find things that work and to persist when it is hard. You may be able to accompany them when they are doing things that they know will trigger anxiety – perhaps if they are challenging fears or simply if the day holds challenges. If you see them getting anxious, remind them of the relaxation skills they have learned and make sure they start to use them *before* their anxiety becomes overwhelming.

Carry hope for them when they cannot

Anxiety is a very frightening emotion. It can feel all-powerful and can make people feel very out of control. Living at the mercy of anxiety can be a demoralizing experience and many people find that they also develop significant problems with depression and feelings of hopelessness. However, it *is* possible to break out of anxiety and get back in control. The most difficult step can be believing that this is true. You can carry that hope for the person you are supporting. Learn about anxiety and learn how to break free from it, and then help them to know that you believe they can do that. Work with them to get the help and support they need to make that a reality, but always let them know that you believe it. On the days when they feel hopeless, they may be unable to believe it themselves, but no matter how low they get, knowing that *you* believe it will be a great strength to them.

Sharing the journey

Working through anxiety is a journey – not just for the sufferer, but for those around them too. Celebrate successes with them, and care for them when things do not go so well. Most of all though, help them to allow themselves time and to face each challenge one at a time. You cannot rush this journey, so take it slowly and do not push for them to transform overnight.

Who cares for the carers?

Finally, do remember to get support yourself. You may not be the one fighting anxiety, but supporting someone else can be tough and place a lot of stress on you. Make sure you have somewhere you can offload that and where you can get support and information. Remember, the more you know, the more effectively you can support someone else.

Useful resources

Charities working with anxiety

Anxiety UK is a national charity based in the UK, run by sufferers and ex-sufferers and supported by a medical advisory panel. They offer support and information for all those affected by anxiety disorders, as well as help in overcoming specific phobias.

www.anxietyuk.org.uk

Telephone helpline 08444 775774 (Monday to Friday, 9.30 a.m. to 5.30 p.m.)

MIND is the leading mental health charity for England and Wales. They work with all mental health conditions, including anxiety, and provide resources and support, as well as campaigning to promote positive mental health.

www.mind.org.uk

Mind*info* Line 0845 766 0163

Online resources using a CBT (cognitive behavioural therapy) approach

The most well-known resources are the Mood Gym http://moodgym.anu.edu.au/welcome and Living Life to the Full http://livinglifetothefull.com.

Both require you to register, but then lead you through a course of CBT.

Relaxation exercises and resources

There are hundreds of books around on relaxation, as well as some that also offer CDs taking you through relaxation exercises step by step. One good way of trying some out without spending a fortune is to borrow them from your local library, which will have copies of the most popular. Alternatively, ask your doctor which they would recommend.

There are also some good resources online. The BBC "headroom" site has a page with some great resources for anxiety, including information on how to do a relaxation exercise, and relaxing tracks to listen to. See http://www.bbc.co.uk/headroom/wellbeing/guides/relaxation.shtml.

Also currently available in the "First Steps" series:

First Steps out of Depression
Sue Atkinson

First Steps out of Eating Disorders
Dr Kate Middleton
and Dr Jane Smith

First Steps out of Problem Drinking
John McMahon

Forthcoming in 2011:

First Steps out of Gambling
Lisa Mills and Joanna Hughes

First Steps through Bereavement
Sue Mayfield